MW01399850

Rom and Ram The Silicon Valley Boys

by
Beverly J. Atwood

DORRANCE PUBLISHING CO., INC
PITTSBURGH, PENNSYLVANIA 15222

Copyright © 1994 by Beverly J. Atwood
All Rights Reserved
ISBN # 0-8059-3538-X
Printed in the United States of America
First Printing

Dedication

To Bruce, my husband and best friend. Thank you for your encouragement and support.

Introduction

Dear reader and seeker of knowledge,

As you read this story, think of it as a riddle or a mystery. How you will solve the mystery is to find the key "code" words that are sprinkled throughout the story. These words are clues. Write down each word that you come to that you think is a clue. After you have finished reading the book, check your key word clue list with the "Key Word Clue List" in the back of the book. The clues are all listed in order of appearance. Read their definitions. How did you do? Did you find all the words? Now read the book over again and see if, with your new-found knowledge, the story takes on a new meaning.

                                        Enjoy solving the mystery.

                                              Beverly J. Atwood

The Silicon Valley was flooding. Boolean families were being separated. Hoping her twin boys, Rom and Ram, could escape the ravages of the rapidly rising water, Queen CPU, their desperate mother, bent from her board and sent them away in a reed boat. She watched as it interfaced with the water, struggled amongst the clogging weeds, and then freed itself and swiftly vanished in the twisting currents.

Unperturbed by all that was happening around them, the two infant brothers sailed on. A cave with a narrow inlet served as the final resting place of the floating craft.

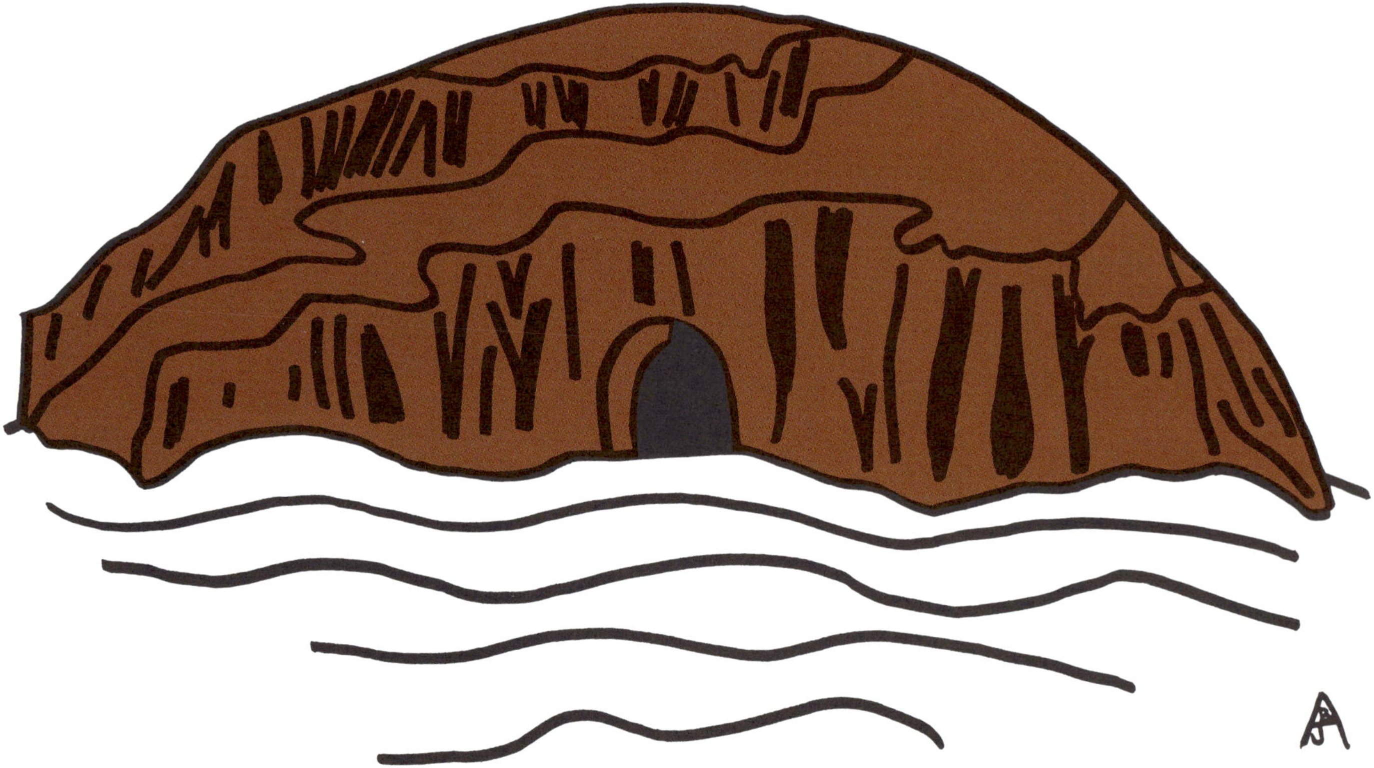

Within the dark walls of the cave lived a wench who, coincidentally, was from the same Boolean Tribe from which the twins had come. She had run away to the caves long before the flood. The cause of her departure was due to her strange appearance. People constantly teased her and called her "Logo."

"Logo," translated from the native language, meant "face of a turtle!"

Therefore she had found her way to the caves to live out her life as a recluse.

However on route to the caves, she had discovered a wounded coyote.

Logo nursed him to health and was rewarded with his friendship. She was happy to have a companion and named him Data.

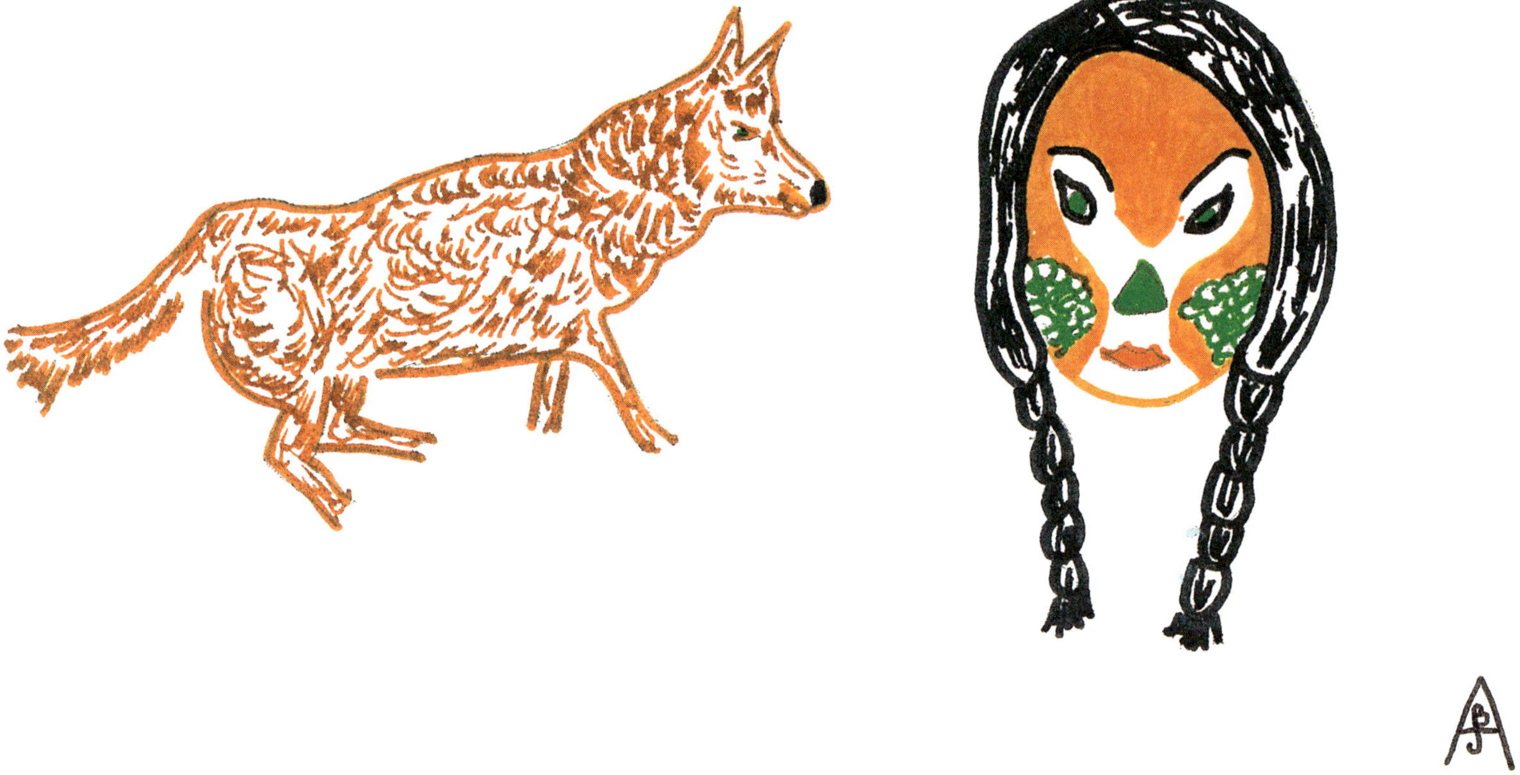

The caves harbored her solitude until the arrival of the floating twins. It was the coyote, Data, who led Logo through the in and out ports of the caves to reveal the presence of the tiny refugees.

She and Data quickly rescued them from their thin raft and warmed and fed them. The twins grew happily in their new surroundings, not really knowing any other life.

Logo knew who the two children were. Data brought all the information and food from the other side of the cave entrance to Logo, therefore keeping her aware of the happenings of the peripheral environment. Data had told Logo that these were the twins of King Computer and Queen CPU.

The wise coyote learned on one of his jaunts out of the cave that the boys were named Rom and Ram.

They all lived through the flood and saw the new sands replace the fallen waters.

Logo had warned the twins, as they grew older, not to venture too far from the cave. But they loved to explore and wondered just to where the valley of sand led.

One day while journeying they tripped over a stone. Much to their shock it spoke to them, telling them that they were the sons of the great King Computer and Queen CPU, who had been lost in a flood years before. Startled, the two boys ran, without looking back, straight to the caves to ask Logo what she knew.

They were reluctantly told by Logo bits and pieces about their heritage. She wished for them to stay with her but, now that they knew of their past, she realized she had to let them go back to claim what was rightfully theirs.

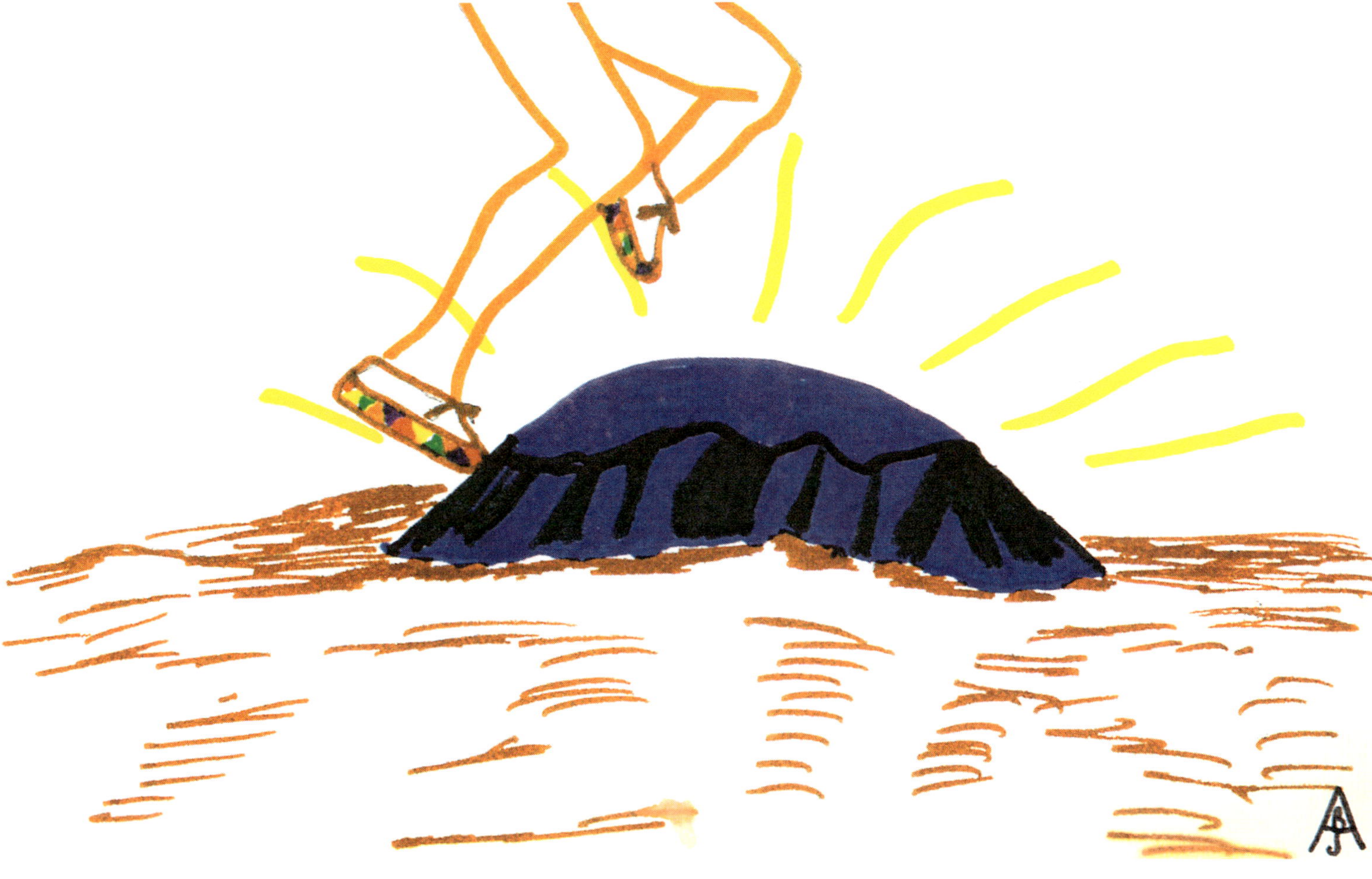

A hollow wooden horse (reminiscent of the description of the Trojan Horse) was made by Rom and Ram from wood that Data had gathered for fires.

They quickly hid inside and had Data pull them to the gates of their former Boolean Village to await dawn.

Alarmed tribe members awoke the next day to view this strange desert beast. As two brave warriors approached and placed their hands on the head of the horse, it bit each hand, leaving an obvious visual display of the bytes.

However neither man felt any pain. They did, oddly enough, recognize that each byte print formed a code that had been used by earlier generations around the time of the great flood. Instantly they decided to run to Chief Abacus. He pondered the nibbled palms of his gate guards, Cursor and Prompt, while stroking his beads.

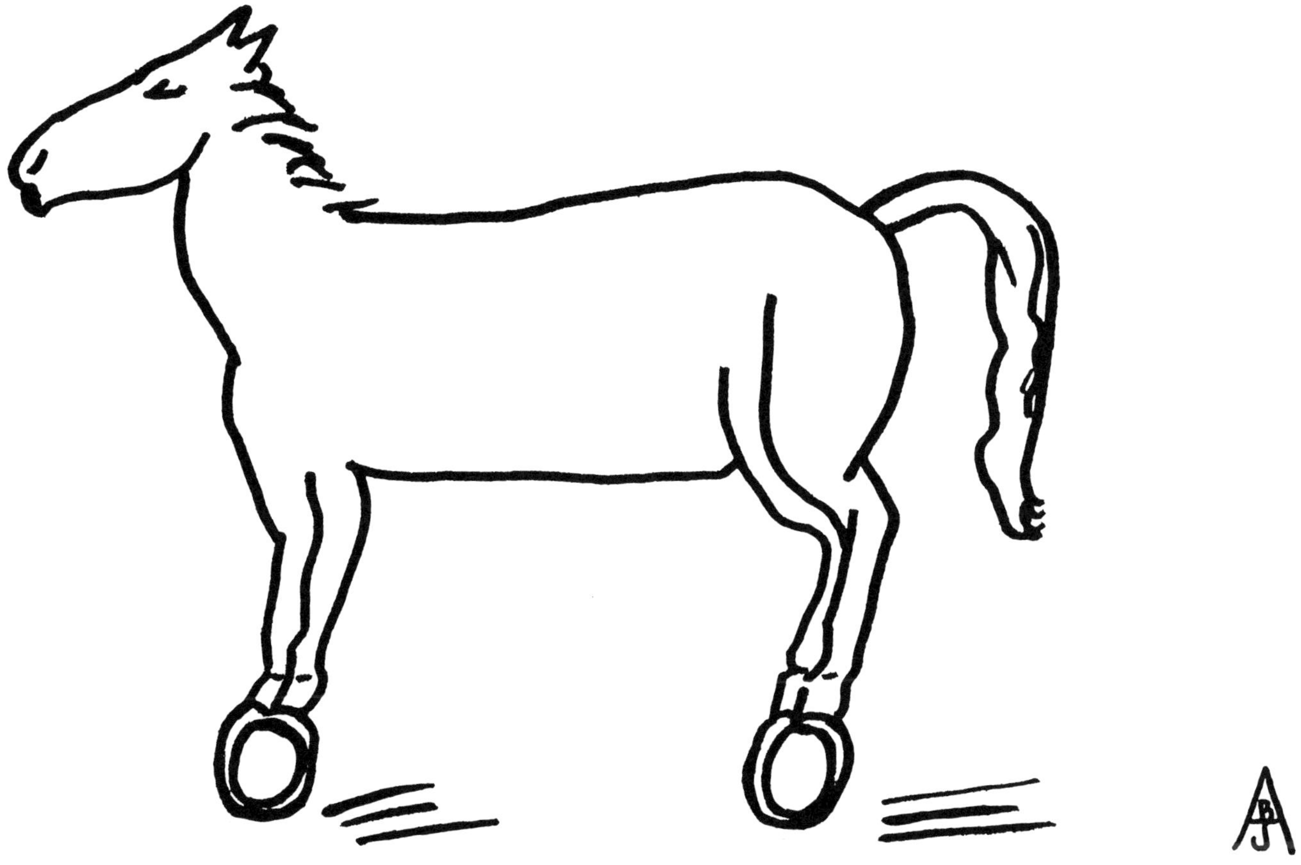

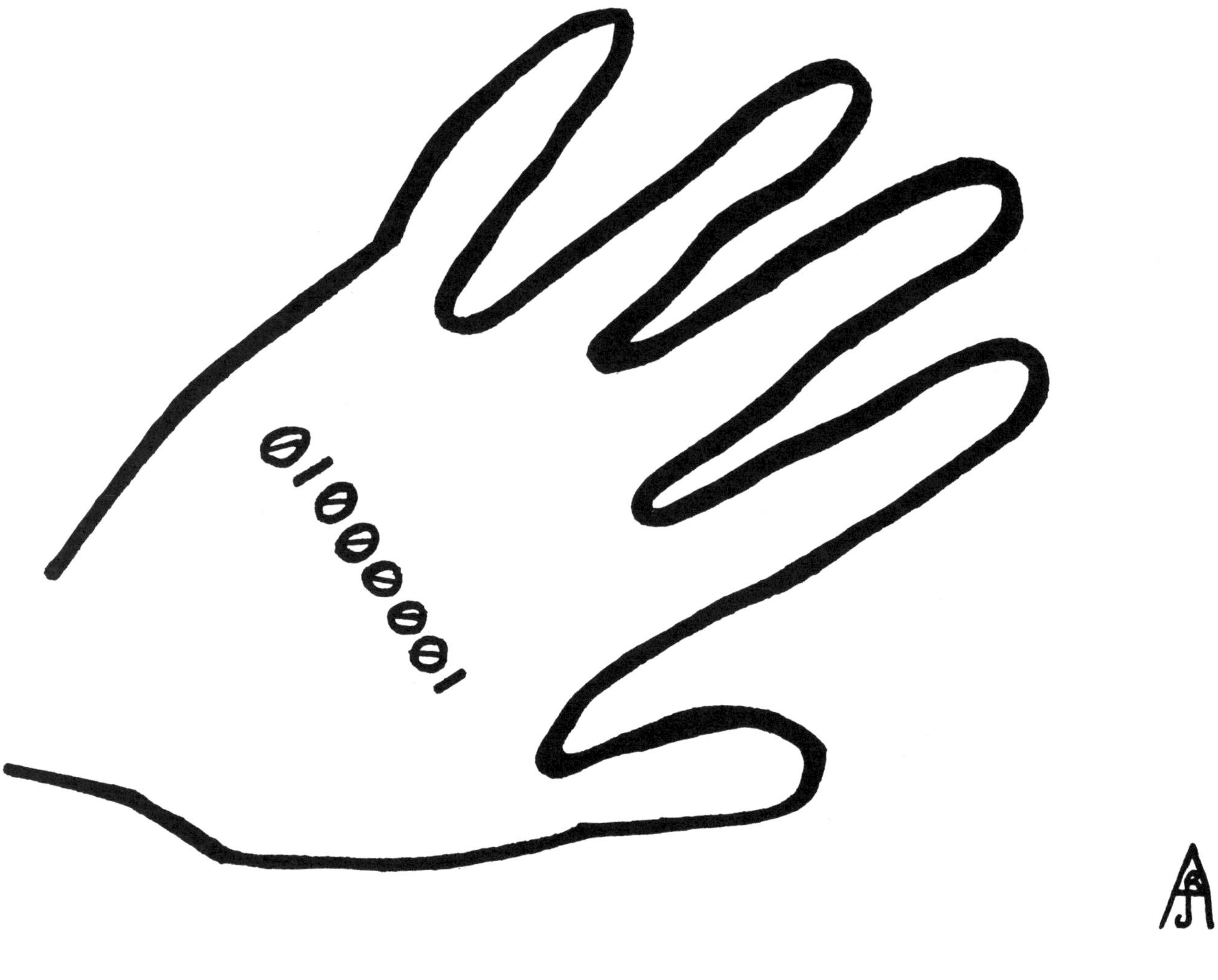
01000001

Then suddenly he wrote in the sand, "Rom and Ram are home."

He paled and excitedly traveled at baud rate speed through the streets to the other side of the village gates to view this array of artificial intelligence.

Noise like a binary signal emitted from the horse. A disk-like door, located in the lower abdomen area, opened, and out jumped the boys Rom and Ram.

Chief Abacus greeted them and led them through the rousing village.

He took them to his cliff dwelling, where he fed them and told them of their true place in the sun.

After the repast, they journeyed up a canyon wall to the top crest, where a huge statue had been erected in honor of King Computer and Queen CPU.

Their memorial overlooked the whole Silicon Valley, where each Boolean Tribe could identify its image against the magnificent skyline.

At the base of the monument, set in the stone, was a riddle. The words were, "If Rom and Ram ever appear, we shall be found."

The mystery of these words had gone unsolved until the moment the twins read the perplexing statement.

Then a heretofore unseen door swung open, leading all into a secret cave.

If Rom and Ram ever appear we shall be found

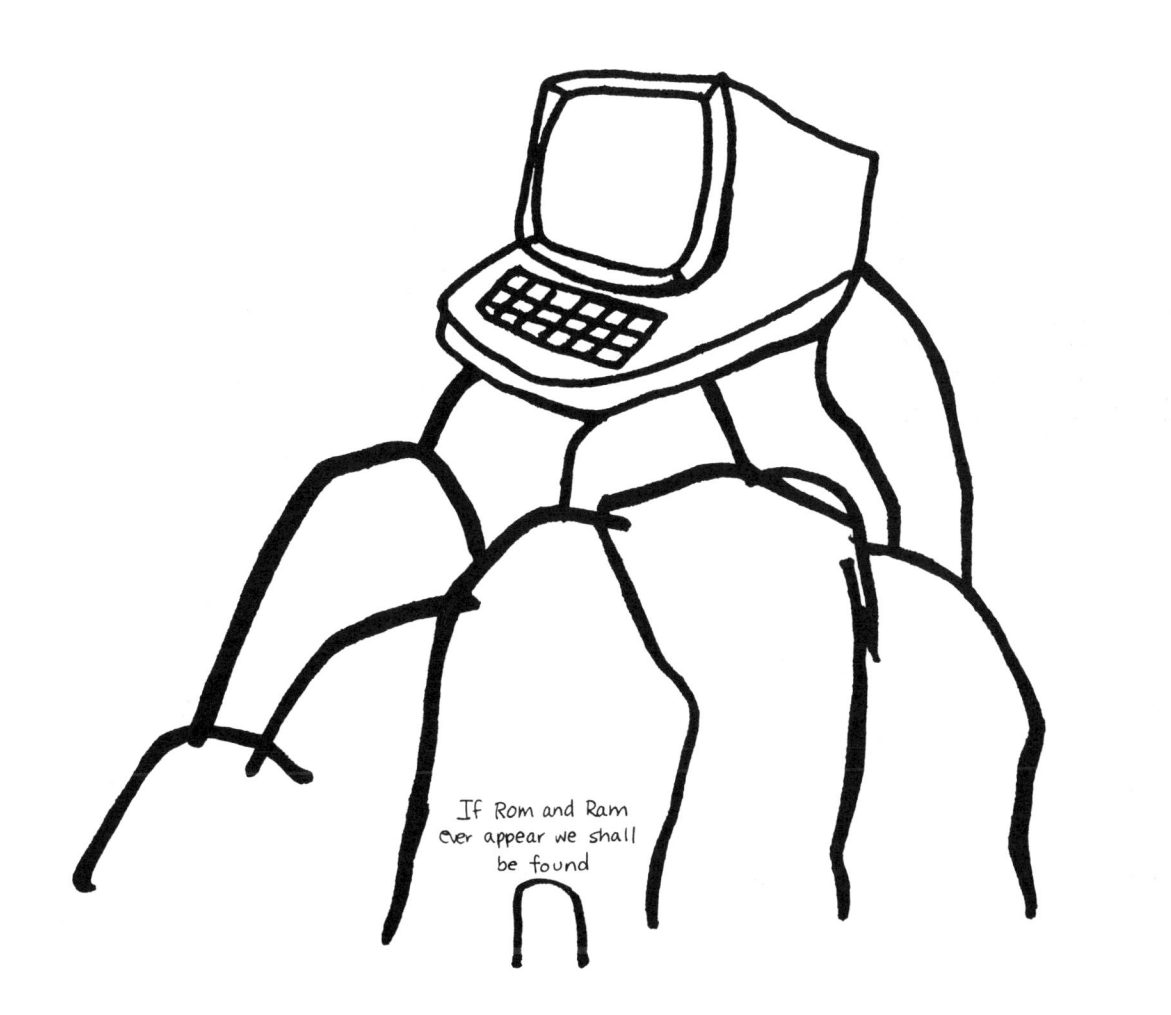

Computer CPU

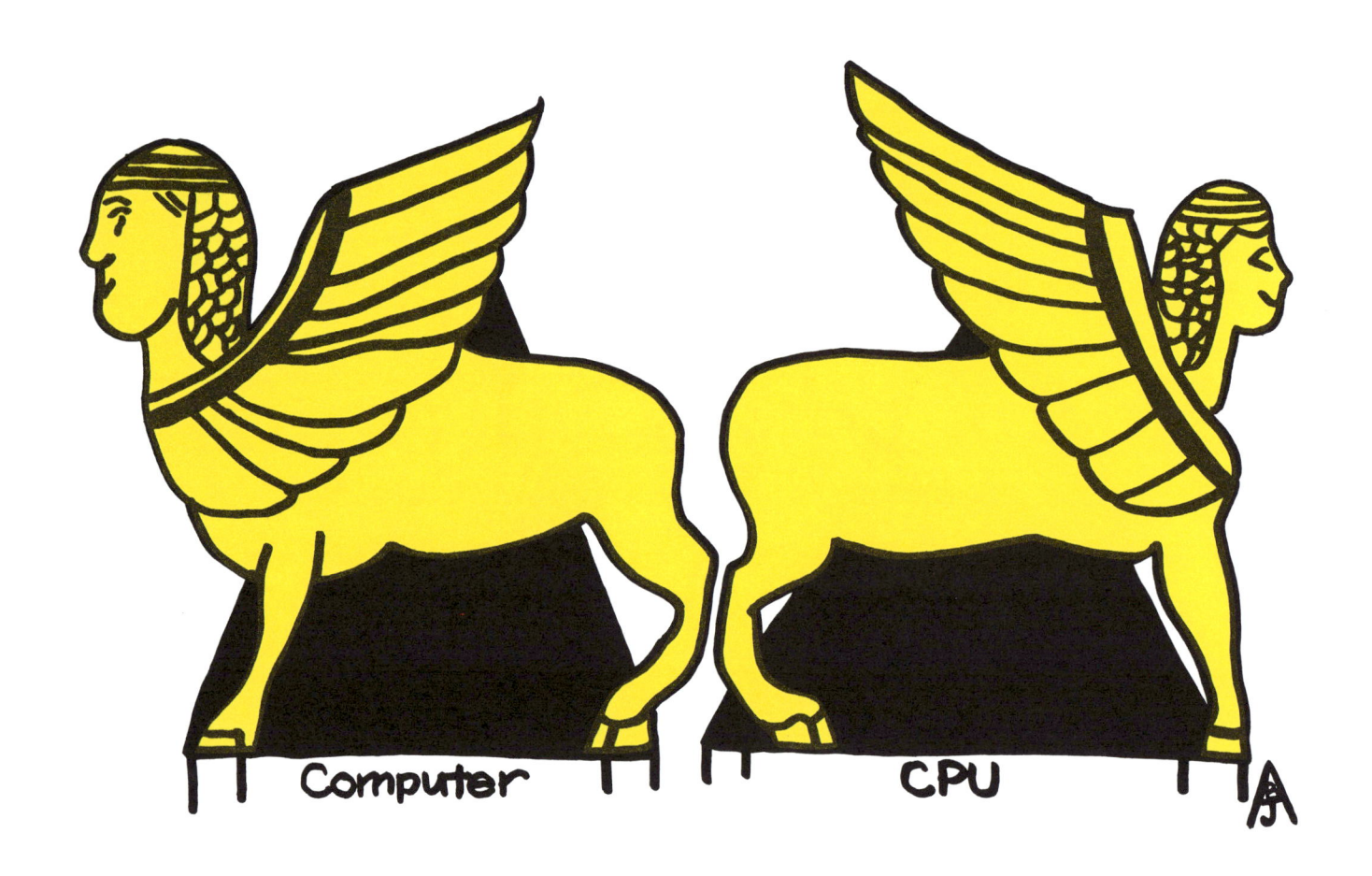

In a state of repose lay King Computer and Queen CPU.

With the excited, volatile nature of Ram and the steady, algorithmic nature of Rom, the parents felt their emotions of joy while in their anesthesia-like state.

But they were unable to be revived until they felt the boot of the boys against their sleeping structures.

Since the time of the flood, King Computer and Queen CPU had been sealed in this hidden tomb.

It was a basic fact to both of them that they just could not function without Rom and Ram.

Therefore they shut down into their self-inflicted exile knowing that they could only be awakened from their catatonic slumber by the boot of their boys.

After emergence from their deferred mode, the king and queen enjoyed a graphic reunion with Rom and Ram.

The boys had returned to the Silicon Valley, forever to reign with their parents, King Computer and Queen CPU.

Without King Computer and Queen CPU, the symbolic language of the land had been reduced to a stick and sand form of communication.

Now the written word was back.

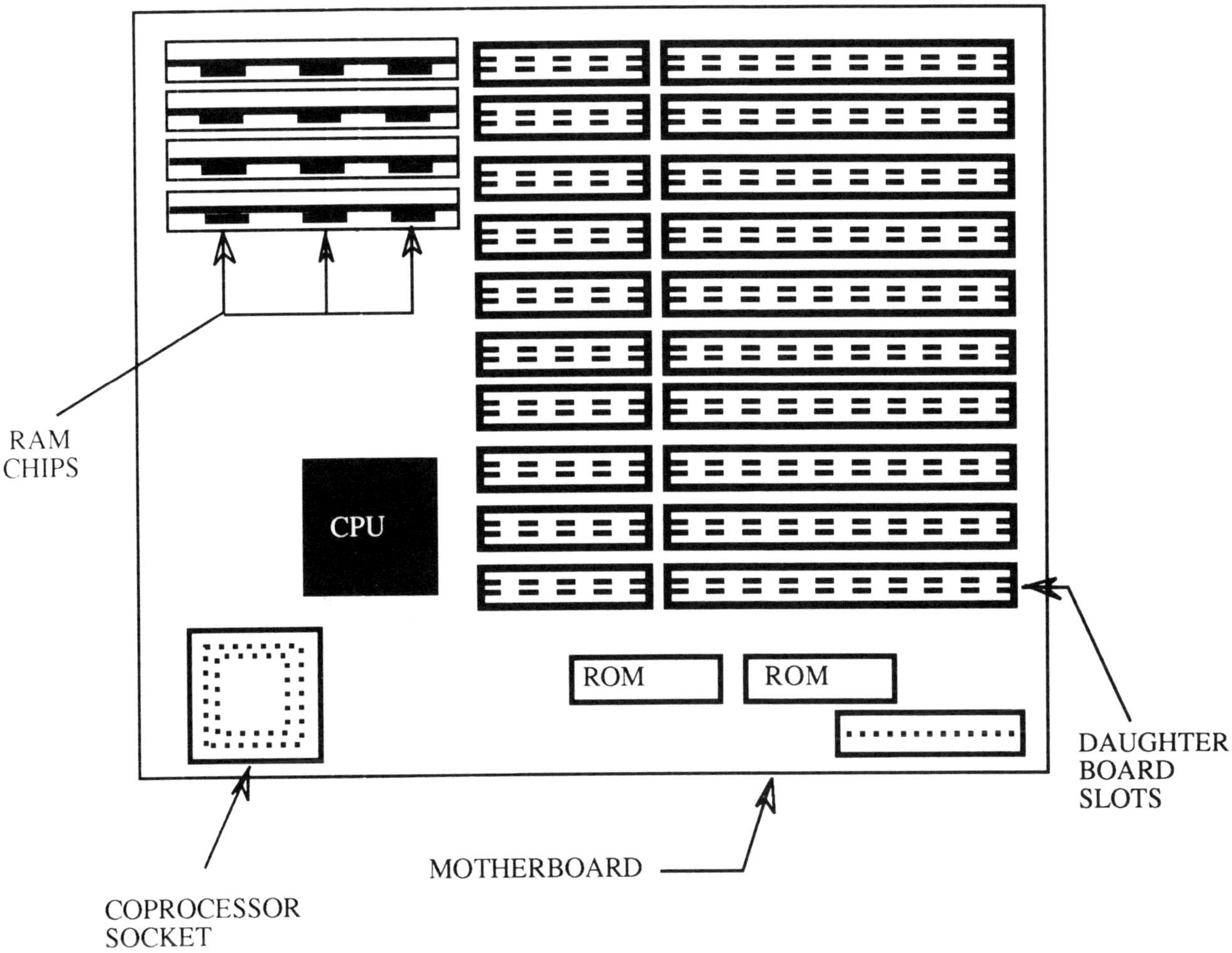
RAM
CHIPS
CPU
ROM
ROM
DAUGHTER
BOARD
SLOTS
MOTHERBOARD
COPROCESSOR
SOCKET

Bibliography

Coburn, Peter; Kelman, Peter; Roberts, Nancy; Snyder, Thomas F.F.; Watt, Daniel H.; Weiner, Cheryl. *Practical Guide to Computers in Education,* Second Edition. Reading, MA: Addison-Wesley Publishing Co., 1985.

Cowan, Les. *The Illustrated Computer Dictionary and Handbook.* San Jose: Enrich/Ohaus Publisher, 1983.

Rice, Jean; Haley, Marien. *My Computer Picture Dictionary.* Minneapolis: T.S. Denison & Co., Inc., 1981.

The End

Thank you for reading this story. I hope it pleased you.

Beverly J. Atwood

Key Word Clue List

(In order of appearance throughout the story)

1. **Rom**
   Story Transalation—A twin son of Queen CPU and King Computer. His memory is alert but he cannot be properly activated without being reconnected with his parents.
   Technical Definition—ROM is an arcanum that means "read only memory". ROM's memory is programmed into the computer, and therefore ROM's stored intelligence remains constant within the computer and thus these facts cannot be altered by the person using the computer.

2. Ram

Story Translation—The other twin son of Queen CPU and King Computer. While separated from his parents he has no memory of them at all.

Technical Definition—RAM is another arcanum and means "random access memory". RAM'S intelligence lasts only as long as the computer is in use. It is a short term memory. When the power is turned off, the intelligence disappears.

3. **Silicon Valley**

Story Translation—A place where a huge quartz rock and sand exist. It is where the boys learned from the rock, a chip of information that led them eventually to a reunion with their computer parents.

Technical Definition—Silicon Valley is located in California. Silicon the element occurs in rocks and sand. Silicon is used in the creation of computer chips. The valley is named after this element because many highly technological computer companies are situated there.

4. **Boolean**

    Story Translation—A group of people who, at one time, had advanced mathematical and communication learning tools. Then came the flood and Rom and Ram were swept away, causing Queen CPU and King Computer to go into exile. The advanced methods of learning were gone.

    Technical Definition—George Boole was an English mathematician who lived from 1815 to 1864. Much of the algebraic logic that he developed then is used in digital computers today.

5. **CPU**

    Story Translation—The queen mother of Rom and Ram. Without her boys she cannot function.

    Technical Definition—CPU is another arcanum. The words "central processing unit" are what the letters stand for. It is in control of the computer's overall activities of intelligence.

6. Mother board

Story Translation—The board Queen CPU bent from to release her boys and set them free to, hopefully, survive the floods.

Technical Definition—The mother board is the prime printed circuit board to which other circuit boards can be wired or attached by plugs.

7. Interface

Story Translation—The twins' little boat interacted with the water. It connected with the water and because of the joining the craft was able to sail.

Technical Definition—Interface is the joining of two separate machines. This union causes them to react. The joining of a computer to a printer causes the computer's visual display to be copied on paper by the interfaced printer.

8. Logo

Story Translation—Logo is the person who saved the twins in the story and educated them while they were under her care.
Technical Definition—Logo is an educational computer program using a turtle symbol throughout.

9. Turtle

Story Translation—The birthmark on Logo's face which caused her to become self-conscious. She thought it drew attention to her.
Technical Definition—Turtle is an attention symbol used in Logo education programs.

10. Data

Story Translation—The name of the coyote who brought the information outside of the cave to Logo.

Technical Definition—Data processed into a computer results in answers and new-found knowledge.

11. In and out ports

Story Translation—The cave entrance is the in port of the cave and the exit is the out port of the cave. From these areas Data linked information from the boys' village to Logo in the cave dwelling.

Technical Definition—In and out ports are the part of the central processing unit (CPU) into which external computer equipment can be plugged.

12. Peripheral environment

Story Translation—The space, area, objects, creatures, and people surrounding the twins.

Technical Definition—Peripheral environment, as associated with a computer, is the interfaced technological apparatuses that surround and are joined to the computer, such as a printer and disk drive.

13. Computer

Story Translation—King Computer in the story cannot function without his twin sons, Rom and Ram. Thus the fact-finding, intelligent, problem-solving computer king had to lay dormant until he was reunited with his boys Rom and Ram.

Technical Definition—Computer is a word that denotes a machine that receives information and, with its stored intelligence, is able to compute or provide an answer.

14. Bit

Story Translation—A small piece of information that helped Rom and Ram understand their origins.

Technical Definition—BIT is an anagram from the word BInary digiT. BInary digiT is a numeral system that uses two numbers as the base. 0 and 1 are used as the binary code in the computer. Bit is a single number of the binary code, or the least amount of information available.

15. Visual display

Story Translation—The story description of visual display is when the horse bit the warrior's hand and thus revealed or showed the secret binary number code.

Technical Definition—Visual display is the actual opportunity to see data exhibited from the computer via a CRT monitor.

16. Byte

Story Translation—The byte from the horse was a binary number code.

Technical Definition—Byte is made up of a formation of binary digits, usually eight. Eight bits make one byte. 01000001 is a byte.

17. Code

Story Translation—The binary number code on the warrior's hand revealed the clue to the identity of Rom and Ram.

Technical Definition—Code is a unit of commands generated for the computer. Binary number code is the system used.

18. Generation

Story Translation—Certain age groups of people are defined as people of a certain time period. They share some like characteristics, such as being the same age. These groups can be classified as the old generation, middle age generation, young and children's generation. The story tells of the older group of people, or generation, as being exposed to a different method of communication.

Technical Definition—Generation, as used in computer terminology, is the use of different kinds of components with which to manufacture computers, for example, equipment that was made in one time zone as opposed to what was considered necessary to use in another era of time. First generation computers function with vacuum tubes.

19. Run

Story Translation—To move swiftly like the warriors did, to run and tell their Chief some important information.

Technical Definition—Run the computer means to operate a program that will give you information.

20. Abacus

Story Translation—Abacus was the Chief who made each thought and act of his life count. He thought out logically how to find Rom and Ram's parents.

Technical Definition—Abacus is a method of counting by using balls or beads that are strung by wire on a frame. It has been used for centuries and was developed by the Chinese.

21. Nibble

Story Translation—The nibbled palms of the warriors were the palms that showed the binary code, or one byte.

Technical Definition—Nibble equals one half of a byte. Therefore one half a byte equals four bits.

22. Cursor

Story Translation—The name of the warrior who directed Abacus to the hollow horse with the concealed twins.

Technical Definition—Cursor is a movable mark on a computer video screen where the next letter or character can be placed.

23. Prompt

Story Translation—The name of the other warrior who brought the message about the hollow horse and instructed Abacus where to go.

Technical Definition—Prompt instructs the computer operator, via a printed message on the computer video screen, what function to operate next.

24. Baud rate

Story Translation—Baud rate was the speed at which Abacus fled to discover what the mystery of the palm codes meant.

Technical Definition—Baud rate is the sum of the number of bits transmitted in one second.

25. Array

Story Translation—The view of the computer monument on the mountain was a clue to the knowledge of the hidden stored information within the cave.

Technical Definition—Array is stored information in the main memory.

26. Artificial Intelligence

Story Translation—The computer monument represented a former generation of human intelligence.

Technical Definition—Artificial intelligence within the computer permits the computer to compute, reason and learn.

27. Binary Signal

Story Translation—The noise emitted from the horse giving out information in code form signalled all to notice the opening of the horse's disk door.

Technical Definition—Binary signal is a code method used through group strands of binary numbers to impart artificial intelligence or information into a computer.

28. Disk

Story Translation—Disk is the door that opened in the hollow horse, releasing the information or knowledge of Rom and Ram's presence.

Technical Definition—Disk is like a round, flat, magnetic record. The computer user slips the small disk into the disk drive, which will then transport the information that has been stored on the disk to the viewer via the computer video screen. The disk is a way to store data. Some disks are hard and others are floppy.

29. Image

Story Translation—The image seen by all on top of the mountain was that of the computer. It was the exact replica of the knowledge the generation of people before the flood had. That same likeness is what they kept stored in their minds when they were away from the monument and unable to view it.

Technical Definition—Image in computer terminology means the reproduction of the same information or memory that is then transmitted to another portion of memory.

30. Read

Story Translation—The twins had to read the riddle at the base of the monument in order to find the way to their memories. Their memories would soon return when they were reunited in a different location with their parents, Queen CPU and King Computer.

Technical Definition—Read from memory transports the data locked in the computer's memory to function in another area. The CPU may receive the data.

31. Volatile

Story Translation—Volatile was the memory of Ram. If he was not with Queen CPU he had no memory at all.

Technical Definition—Volatile memory is like a balloon with air in it. Puncture a balloon and the air will come out, thus the balloon will not be able to float. When the power of a computer is shut off, the memory part called RAM loses all of the information it had stored in it. RAM's volatile memory only works when the computer is on.

32. Algorithmic

Story Translation—Algorithmic was the steady logical memory of Rom while trying to energize his parents, Queen CPU and King Computer.

Technical Definition—Algorithmic is a system of arithmetic that engages in solving a specific problem, in a circumscribed number of logical steps.

33. Boot

Story Translation—To boot their computer parents and thus revive them into action is what Rom and Ram were trying to do.
Technical Definition—Boot a computer is to make it react to a set of instructions either from an inserted program or by simply switching the computer on.

34. Structure

Story Translation—The formally structured forms of King Computer and Queen CPU with which Rom and Ram were uniting.
Technical Definition—Structure is an orderly, methodical, and systematic method of formulating a computer program.

35. Basic

Story Translation—The basic fact about the Computer King and Queen CPU was that they could not function without Rom or Ram.

Technical Definition—Basic is another arcanum that translates to Beginner's All-purpose Symbolic Instruction Code. It is an uncomplicated language.

36. Deferred Mode

Story Translation—Deferred mode refers to the sleeping condition that King Computer and Queen CPU were in before they awoke, where they rested before they could be activated into action.

Technical Definition—Deferred mode is the ability to write a program into the computer's memory bank, and then delay the use of the program by storing it on a disk.

37. Graphic

Story Translation—Graphic reunion with the twins meant that King Computer and Queen CPU were in full working capacity now that they were reunited with Rom and Ram. They could execute a program that displayed their joy and happiness through pictures and letters on the computer monitor screen.

Technical Definition—Graphic computer activity is the visual display of any program that instructs the computer to draw letters, charts, designs, and pictures.

38. Language

Story Translation—The symbolic language of the computer was now found. The people of the Boolean Village would once again be able to advance their civilization to new levels. The exciting resurrection of the computer put a feeling of power and creativity into many who wished to now write computer programs.

Technical Definition—Language is the term used to denote the special group of symbols, rules, letters, and numbers used to write computer programs.

39. Communication

Story Translation—The communication is regenerated through the computer to the entire Boolean country.

Technical Definition—Communication is a method of networking data from one terminal to another, such as Prodigy and Internet.